THE GRAND TOUR

Mike Rendell

SHIRE PUBLICATIONS

Bloomsbury Publishing Plc

Kemp House, Chawley Park, Cumnor Hill, Oxford OX2 9PH, UK

29 Earlsfort Terrace, Dublin 2, Ireland

1385 Broadway, 5th Floor, New York, NY 10018, USA

E-mail: shire@bloomsbury.com

www.shirebooks.co.uk

SHIRE is a trademark of Osprey Publishing Ltd

First published in Great Britain in 2022

ISBN: PB 978 1 78442 495 4
        eBook 978 1 78442 498 5
        ePDF 978 1 78442 496 1
        XML 978 1 78442 497 8

22 23 24 25 26   10 9 8 7 6 5 4 3 2 1

Typeset by PDQ Digital Media Solutions, Bungay, UK

Printed and bound in India by Replika Press Private Ltd

Shire Publications supports the Woodland Trust, the UK's leading woodland conservation charity.

COVER IMAGE
Front cover: Detail of Canaletto's *Entrance to the Grand Canal* (Museum of Fine Arts, Houston/ Public Domain). Back cover: Fourth-century Roman medallion (Metropolitan Museum, New York/Public Domain).

TITLE PAGE IMAGE
A painting by Willey Reveley of ruins in Rome, *c.*1785.

CONTENTS PAGE IMAGE
A marble sarcophagus brought back to England by the Duke of Beaufort in 1733 and displayed at Badminton House (now on show at the Metropolitan Museum, New York).

DEDICATION
To Philippa: my guide through time.

ACKNOWLEDGEMENTS

Images are gratefully acknowledged as follows:

alh1/CC BY-ND 2.0, page 42; Author's collection, pages 10 (bottom), 11 (bottom); Huntington Library, Pasadena/Public Domain, page 19; Lewis Walpole Library/Public Domain, pages 5 (bottom), 7 (both), 10 (top), 12 (bottom), 52, 60; Library of Congress/ Public Domain, page 50; Mark Goodger Antiques, pages 27, 55; Metropolitan Museum, New York/Public Domain, pages 3, 6 (both), 8, 11 (top), 12 (top left and right), 14 (top), 15, 18, 23, 24, 25 (both), 26, 28 (both), 29, 30 (top), 32, 37, 38 (top), 39 (both), 40, 46, 47 (both), 49, 54 (bottom), 56–7, 59; Museum of Fine Arts, Houston/Public Domain, page 14 (bottom); Photo by VCG Wilson/Corbis via Getty Images, page 16–17; Smithsonian Design Museum/Public Domain, page 54 (top); Towneley Hall Art Gallery and Museum/Bridgeman Images, page 20; Wikimedia courtesy of University of Texas/Public Domain, page 5 (top); Yale Center for British Art/Public Domain, pages 1, 13, 30 (bottom), 33 (top), 34–5, 36, 38 (bottom left), 38 (bottom right), 41, 44 (both), 45 (both), 48.

CONTENTS

INTRODUCTION

IT HAS BEEN called a rite of passage – a sort of gap-year for the nobility. In reality the Grand Tour usually lasted for several years, and was a sort of 'finishing school' for aristocrats, giving them a more rounded education. For some it was a chance to 'sow wild oats' before settling down. For many, it was a Continental booze-up, a prolonged itinerary of excessive consumption, gambling and sexual experimentation. For others it was a chance to experience European culture and ideas, polish up their foreign language skills, encounter beautiful paintings, architecture and *objets d'art* and then to return home with souvenirs with which they filled their newly built country homes.

The term 'Grand Tour' was first used in a travel guide published in 1670. At that stage it was reserved for aristocrats finishing their education, but as time went on it broadened its appeal to include a whole army of tourist-painters, collectors, aspiring architects and classical scholars. From 1800, increasing numbers of women completed their version of the Grand Tour and the length of the typical tour dropped from perhaps four years to an average of two years.

The Tour promoted an industry built around the needs of the tourists, particularly in Paris and in Rome. In Britain it gave employment to tutors, known as 'bear leaders' or ciceroni, who had the thankless task of accompanying the Grand Tourists while trying to keep their charges on the straight and narrow.

OPPOSITE
A Travelling Tutor and a Monkey Child. Scenes showing monkeys engaged in human activities – *singeries* in French – were traditional in the seventeenth and eighteenth centuries, reflecting an uncomplimentary view of the Grand Tourist.

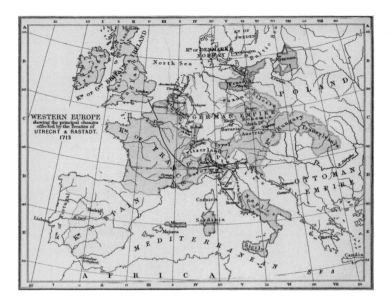

Map of Europe from 1700 showing national boundaries and, in red, the route taken on a typical Grand Tour through France and Italy.

On the Continent it boosted hotels, restaurants and *pensions* (lodging houses). It brought wealth and employment all along the route, traditionally to Paris, down to Lyon, and across the Alps. From Turin to Venice, then on to Florence, Rome and Naples, the tourists brought traffic chaos – and money.

Above all, the Grand Tour helped broaden the mind and complete the education of a great many highly privileged and influential young men. Never before had so many members of the ruling class been so close to European culture and Continental influences.

The Tour gave a boost to antiquarians and to the excavations at Herculaneum, which started in 1738, and at Pompeii, discovered in 1748. It provided an outlet for a small army of artists such as Canaletto, churning out scenes which would be

A TRAVELLING TUTOR and a MONKEY CHILD

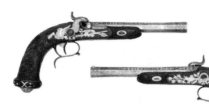

chosen by the tourists as mementos of their tour. It generated an outlet for artefacts from Rome and Ancient Greece, as well as providing employment for unscrupulous copyists and fakers. It led to a revival in classical styles, influencing designers and architects who then developed those ideas back in Britain. And it provided inspiration for hundreds of artists who helped feed a mania for all things Italian. As a side effect, the Tour was a gigantic exercise in networking, because the people completing their Grand Tour frequently did so in a sort of itinerant herd, often sticking together, conversing solely in English and reducing encounters with the locals to an absolute minimum as they swept like locusts from one cultural centre to the next.

The Tour resulted in some extraordinary male fashions. Men were nicknamed 'macaronis' – a derogatory reference to anything Italian – if they wore ludicrously high, heavily

Pair of French pistols, 1829. Duelling was illegal in Britain but that would not have deterred tourists from bringing back a pair of pistols.

Canaletto's view of Campo Sant' Angelo in Venice.

powdered wigs, or followed the trend for tight trousers, or walked with a dandified swagger.

The Grand Tour really got going after 1660. Of course, before that time people had travelled abroad as tourists, but with the restoration of the monarchy a well-trodden path developed, focusing on Paris and Rome. It reached its heyday during the 1760s and was still in full swing until 1789. The French Revolution was followed by a deterioration in Anglo–French relations, to say nothing of the risk of a noble tourist losing his head. Travellers could still set off from Dover for Ostend and from there travel through Germany, Austria and Switzerland and down into Italy. However, when Napoleon invaded Italy in 1796 that country also became out of bounds. Some adapted their tour to include Greece and the rest of the Ottoman Empire, travelling as far as Egypt, but for many the Tour was suspended until peace in Europe was restored by the Treaty of Paris in 1815.

When it re-commenced, the Tour to France and Italy had started to go down-market, attracting tourists on a cut-down version, and by the middle of the nineteenth century the advent of the train had led to the birth of mass tourism; the Grand Tour as an exclusive aristocratic venture was effectively over.

HOW D'YE LIKE ME.

How d'ye like me? by Carington Bowles, 1772, showing the affected dress of an English macaroni, imitating Continental fashions.

English visitors standing out like a sore thumb among Parisiennes in 1825.

ALONG THE WAY

WHEREAS A TRAVELLER on the Grand Tour had a huge variety of choices – how long to stay away, where to visit, what route to take, how much to spend – there were certain things all travellers had to contend with, and the first of these was crossing the English Channel. The usual route was from Dover to either Calais or Boulogne and the crossing could be a nightmare if the seas were rough. On arrival, after a voyage of perhaps 36 hours cooped up in considerable discomfort, the tourist had to contend with the delay and indignity of having all belongings searched by over-zealous customs officials. It was a ritual which they would have to contend with many times, especially in Italy as they passed from one principality to the next. The traveller would need a passport. From 1778 these were written in French (the language of diplomacy) and had to be signed personally by the monarch. After 1794 they were signed by the Secretary of State.

Then there were the roads, often in appalling condition, especially in Germany. In Britain, roads had improved significantly by the 1760s, thanks to funding under the various Turnpike Acts, but Continental roads were often deeply rutted and sometimes impassable in bad weather. The wealthy traveller might have his own carriage, with his own coach driver and servants to look after him; the poorer tourist had to contend with public transport. In an average day the driver might cover 15 to 20 miles, depending on conditions.

OPPOSITE
Detail from
J.M.W. Turner's
view entitled *The
Fort of L'Esseillon*,
1835, showing the
heavily fortified
route to the
Mont Cenis Pass
(see page 13).

The Landing of John Bull at Boulogne by James Gillray, 1792.

The traveller would never trust local doctors and would need to be self-sufficient in terms of medical supplies, so would have his own travelling medicine box. He would need a pistol, to defend himself from armed robbers. He would need a travelling clock, a telescope and a travelling canteen. He would also need a travel guide such as the 1722 *Gentleman's Pocket Companion for Travelling into Foreign Parts* or Thomas Nugent's *Grand Tour*, first published in 1743. Those wanting a cut-down tour might choose the 1750 *A Five Weeks Tour to Paris*, being an eighteenth-century equivalent of a 'Rough Guide' to the horrors of French travel.

Once on French soil the tourist would have to contend with the overnight stops at various inns *en route* to Paris. The general complaint was about the dire food, the foul wine, the surly innkeepers, and about bedsheets which had never been aired and felt damp. As one guidebook put it: 'I have

An eighteenth-century paper cut-out showing a horse-drawn carriage about to crash down over a huge boulder.

actually catched them in France about to sheet a bed with Linnen almost what we call wringing wet.'

Typically, a visitor would reckon to spend a couple of months in the French capital, and one of his first priorities would be to obtain local currency. A network of correspondent banks flourished across the Continent, willing to accept letters of credit. If the traveller wanted to avoid being robbed, he would have to avoid keeping large amounts of cash. By and large, gold was a universal currency, and an English sovereign would be just as acceptable as a French Louis d'Or, but for everyday living, coins in lower denominations were essential.

In Paris, the new arrival would commission a complete new wardrobe of clothes and would spend several hours every day practising French; he might also be taught fencing and dancing skills.

Travelling clock made in London in 1713. It features an alarm, a calendar, and has a universal joint beneath the hanging loop, to cushion jolting movements.

Stand and Deliver! Paper cut-out from c.1780. Grand Tourists carrying all their luggage and acquisitions were obvious targets for thieves, especially in remote areas.

Armed with his guidebook the traveller would then have been free to explore the delights of Paris. He would have been warned to avoid the local wine, on account of 'the great looseness' which this might cause. According to one book, 'no Place in the elegant or delicate World is so ill-provided with Conveniences for such a condition as Paris is.'

Gold was always welcome and interchangeable. On the left a double Sovereign of George III dated 1820. On the right, a double Louis d'Or dated 1755.

He would visit churches such as Notre Dame and the church of the Val-de-Grâce, or palaces such as the Palais Royal, home to the Duc d'Orléans ('the Collection of Pictures is the best in France'). He would visit the Louvre and promenade in the Tuileries ('the most magnificent gardens in Paris'). In time he might venture south towards Versailles to view the royal palace.

The wealthy tourist might buy a new carriage in Paris, intending to sell it at the end of the journey. Poorer travellers would make a four-day trip, in a coach known as a 'diligence', down to Lyon. From Lyon the intrepid traveller would have a choice: head down to Marseilles and take a chance with the Barbary pirates on the sea crossing to Italy; or continue by road and face the horrors of the Alpine crossing.

Crossing the Alps into Italy usually meant heading for the Mont Cenis Pass, near the Val d'Isère. Here the terrors of the journey really started. Tourists with their own carriages would have them dismantled and taken by mule train along mountain paths. The tourists would have a barely more dignified ride on an Alp-machine, which was a sort of sedan chair strapped to carrying poles, carried shoulder-high by porters. Having reached the summit, the party would then begin a hair-raising descent on what was basically a sled, hurtling down towards the plains of Piedmont and the city of Turin. This was merely a stop on the way to the four cities which demanded attention: Venice, Florence, Rome and Naples.

Thomas Rowlandson's picture of the Paris diligence.

OPPOSITE, BOTTOM
H.W. Bunbury's 1767 *Englishman at Paris*.

OVERLEAF, TOP
Elaborately decorated carriage design, seventeenth to eighteenth century.

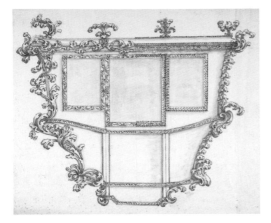

Venice was famous then, as now, for its Carnival. But this was no one-week wonder and could last from Boxing Day to Shrove Tuesday. It meant a non-stop round of masquerades, visits to the opera, firework displays, music – and courtesans. Venice as a trading power was past its prime, but the English saw it as a quintessential Renaissance city and flung themselves into the full range of worldly pursuits with all the strength they could muster. If they had the stamina, they would still be there in May to witness the celebrations marking Ascension Day. This involved much pomp and ceremony, with a festival on the water signifying the maritime supremacy of the city state of Venice.

Canaletto's
*Entrance to the
Grand Canal.*

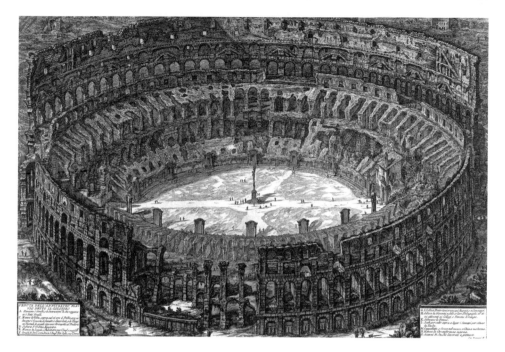

Small wonder that by the time he reached Florence the exhausted Grand Tourist saw it as a place to relax and unwind – and visit the countless art galleries, churches and palaces exhibiting paintings, the likes of which he had never seen in Britain. So, the tourists would have copies made, and parcel them up to be sent back to Britain.

Piranesi's amazingly detailed birds-eye view of the Colosseum, 1776.

No trip to Florence was complete without a visit to the Uffizi Gallery. The Uffizi was one of the world's first modern museums, housing the art collection gathered by the Medici banking family after it came to prominence during the first half of the fifteenth century. The gallery had originally been opened to visitors only by prior appointment, but in 1765 it was officially opened to the public and was an absolute 'must see' for the Grand Tourists.

OVERLEAF
Zoffany's *Tribuna of the Uffizi* was painted over a six-year period from 1772.

The Tribuna, an octagonal room stacked high with Renaissance masterpieces, became a meeting place for British tourists who saw themselves as art connoisseurs. Here they

Panini's *Modern Rome*, 1757, which cleverly shows the famous monuments of the city as paintings displayed in an imaginary gallery.

would meet with friends, take tea, admire the paintings and display their knowledge of great art.

Having re-charged the batteries in Florence it was time to head for Rome. Here, the tourist would engage the services of a local antiquarian to show him the glories of the Eternal City. He would tick off the Colosseum, the Pantheon, St Peter's Basilica and the Roman Forum. He would spend time in the local churches admiring the paintings, visit the Sistine Chapel and perhaps venture a little inland to see the ruined villa of the Emperor Hadrian. Some tourists would have their portraits painted by leading local artists such as Pompeo Batoni, who specialised in English *milordi* to the extent that 175 out of the 225 known portraits painted by him are of British subjects. Others with lesser means preferred to purchase a caricature likeness by Pier Leone Ghezzi as a memento of their visit.

They purchased etchings of *vedute* (views) by local artists such as Giovanni Battista Piranesi. Some tried their hand at drawing and painting, while many opened their purse strings and bought souvenirs or invested in sculptures and *objets d'art* from antiquity.

The next stop after Rome involved travelling down to the Kingdom of Naples. Here, between 1764 and 1800, Sir William Hamilton was the British Ambassador. Sir William was a fanatical collector – of paintings, sculptures and antiquities from both Ancient Greece and the Roman Empire – and as such he was a conduit for other collectors because he could source whatever the discerning tourist was looking for.

Visitors could combine Naples with a trip to observe the excavations around Pompeii, or climb the lower slopes of Mount Vesuvius, perhaps waiting until nightfall to observe the periodic explosions. Visiting artists, such as Turner and Joseph Wright, were spellbound by the awesome power of nature and repeatedly painted the erupting volcano.

Vesuvius from Portici by Joseph Wright of Derby. Wright visited the area between 1773 and 1775. In practice, the volcano did not erupt during this period of time, so the scene was either imagined or copied.

FROM THE GREAT COLLECTORS ...

ONE OF BRITAIN'S earliest great collectors, Hans Sloane, was not so much a product of the Grand Tour as a medical student who finished his university studies in Paris and Montpellier. Shortly after his return to England in 1685 he was elected as a member of the Royal Society and became physician to the royal family. Subsequently he travelled to Jamaica to become personal physician to the island's governor.

Throughout this time abroad he collected plant specimens – and also all manner of knick-knacks and curious objects. In the seventeenth century it had become standard for educated gentlemen to have what was known as 'a cabinet of curiosities' containing everything from historical artefacts to fossils, medals and natural specimens. During his lifetime Sloane had acquired many such collections when they came up for sale.

Sloane was a magpie and by the time he handed over his collection to the nation, to form the backbone of the British Museum when it opened in 1759, it consisted of some 71,000 items, many of them never catalogued. This was to be the nucleus around which many of the later Grand Tour collections would coalesce, making the British Museum not just the first public museum in the world, but also one which housed some of the most significant records of culture and human endeavour.

Initially, visitors to the Museum had to apply in advance for a timed ticket, and go round in escorted tours, but in time this requirement was relaxed.

OPPOSITE
Johann Zoffany's 1782 portrait of Charles Towneley in his Sculpture Gallery. Towneley is shown in the foreground, to the right, with his friends the politician Charles Greville, Thomas Astle, conservator of the British Museum, and Pierre d'Hancarville, French antiquarian, in the background.

For some, the Grand Tour was an opportunity to buy the odd souvenir, but for a few it was to set the Tourist on a lifetime of collecting, an obsession which led men to want the most comprehensive or most significant collection in the world. One such Tourist was Charles Towneley, who made repeated tours to southern Italy and Sicily in the mid-eighteenth century. He amassed what became known as the Towneley Marbles, which he exhibited in a sculpture gallery in his London home. He was a true connoisseur, and his sculptures were of the finest quality. The collection passed after Towneley's death in 1805 to the British Museum.

Another Grand Tourist was Towneley's close friend Richard Charles Payne, whose four-year tour of Italy lasted between 1772 and 1776. He developed a fascination for ancient art and in particular with small artefacts. His magnificent collections of bronzes, coins, marble sculptures and engraved gems eventually found their way to the British Museum, where Payne was a trustee. When he died in 1824 his collection, including drawings by Raphael, Rembrandt and Rubens, was bequeathed to the Museum.

Another friend of Towneley was Henry Blundell, who toured Italy in 1776. Blundell had a scatter-gun approach to collecting and returned from the Tour with a bulk purchase of eighty marble figures acquired through the agency of Henry Jenkins, a man who had settled in Rome after visiting the city during a Grand Tour in 1750. In the intervening 25 years Jenkins had become a *cicerone* or guide, was a money lender to visiting aristocrats, became a spy for the British government – and was a dealer in antiquities. He was also notorious for ripping off collectors by charging astronomically high commissions.

For Blundell, quantity rather than quality was what mattered. He was perfectly willing to 'improve' his sculptures by getting local craftsmen to make his sculptures more acceptable to contemporary tastes and he never allowed his lack of a deep knowledge of ancient art to get in the way of collecting. He quickly amassed the biggest collection in the country, building a Garden Temple and a mini-Pantheon in order to house the collection at his home, Ince Blundell Hall at Sefton in Merseyside. Whereas the house is now a care home, his collection is largely spread between museums in the Liverpool area.

In a different class, Sir William Hamilton was an avid collector, but one who lacked the deep pockets needed to fund a truly great collection. It was an all-consuming hobby, which led him to become a member of the Society of Dilettanti, open to people who had visited the Ottoman Empire. His scholarly approach eventually led to 'vase-mania' back in Britain, not least when the Portland Vase, acquired by him in the 1780s, passed to the British Museum. Hamilton also collected gems, bronzes and other *objets d'art* and the breadth of his knowledge meant that he was often consulted as an expert by tourists wanting an assessment of what to buy and what to avoid.

Another major collector of sculptures was Sir Richard Worsley, 7th Baronet, who filled his house at Appuldurcombe on the Isle of Wight with antiques, intent on amassing the most important collection of sculptures in the country. His obsession cost him his marriage to the very much younger and somewhat flighty Seymour Worsley, who allegedly embarked on affairs with no fewer than twenty-seven lovers. Sir Richard was humiliated after a very public divorce case but carried on building his collection.

Sir Richard died in 1805, and his house at Appuldurcombe remains as a shell, having suffered bomb damage in the Second World War. Ironically, his dream was never realised: Thomas Bruce, better known to posterity as the 7th Earl of Elgin, trumped his collection

The Portland Vase, a copy made by Sir Josiah Wedgwood.

The Hope Dionysos, a Roman copy of a Greek bronze, acquired by Thomas Hope during one of his extensive Grand Tours. The Hope diamond was another acquisition he made, along with an entire collection of vases purchased from Sir William Hamilton.

by bringing back the Parthenon Marbles, held by the British Museum since 1816.

One other collector of note was Sir Horace Walpole, younger son of Sir Robert Walpole, Britain's first Prime Minister. At the age of 22 he set off on a Grand Tour, returning in 1741. He was imbued with a love of collecting, and six years later bought a small villa in Twickenham. He added turrets, cloisters and battlements and made it into a whimsical concoction of architectural styles, a joyful pseudo-Gothic fantasy which pre-dated the Gothic Revival style.

He filled the library with his collections, specialising in miniatures and small artefacts. Miniature portraits had not previously been considered important, but he amassed a collection of over 130 examples, painted on ivory, bone or vellum. He collected exquisite enamels, arms and armour, Greek pottery and Renaissance majolica. He purchased Holbein drawings and works by contemporary artists such as Sir Joshua Reynolds and the sculptress Anne Damer. When the collections were finally dispersed in 1842, nearly half a century after Sir Horace had died, the items were bought by various museums scattered across the whole world, from Berlin to Australia and the United States. The house at Strawberry Hill remains as a fascinating memorial, albeit hemmed in by a more modern structure built as a teacher training college.

One other great collector was the architect Sir John Soane, who built up one of the most astonishing and eclectic collections at his home, made by knocking together three houses at 13 Lincoln's Inn Fields. It is open to the public as the Soane Museum and contains architectural fragments, sculptures, porcelain, bronzes and manuscripts, together with the sarcophagus of Seti I. Soane also collected paintings by contemporary artists, while his library, running to more than 7,700 volumes, covered a wide range of topics including Greek and Roman classics, poetry, painting, sculpture, history, music, drama and philosophy, as well as topographical works. In addition, he amassed some 30,000 architectural drawings – his own, as well as some by Sir Christopher Wren and by the Adam brothers, Robert and James.

A fourth-century gold glass medallion with mother and child, acquired by Horace Walpole and exhibited at Strawberry Hill until 1842.

He had originally gone on the Grand Tour with the aid of a scholarship provided by the Royal Academy, to the sum of £180 plus travel expenses. This was intended to cover a three-year tour, but Soane returned after two years, in 1780, some £120 in debt. During the tour he had spent time in Rome accurately measuring and drawing many of the ancient buildings, including the Colosseum, before moving on to Naples. From there he travelled down to Sicily where he studied the Ancient Greek ruins which are still standing in many parts of the island.

Thomas Rowlandson's *Italian Picture Dealers humbuging My Lord Anglaise.*

In his lifetime his seemingly haphazard display of his collections baffled visitors but they remain on display, exactly as Soane had left them, nearly two centuries after his death in 1837. They fill every nook and cranny of his home, a testament to an extraordinary man who had a special role to play in promoting the neoclassical style of architecture.

... TO THE SOUVENIR HUNTERS

Q UITE APART FROM the collectors who devoted their entire lives to the study and acquisition of ancient art, there were thousands of wealthy aristocrats wanting to buy a souvenir of their foreign travels. This sparked a whole new industry: what the Italians were not able to dig out of the ground, they manufactured in back-street potteries and metal-working shops.

Fakes abounded, but in addition there was a huge demand for objects which simply reminded the visitor of his time abroad. Examples would be the fans, often decorated with pictures of the Colosseum, or Vesuvius, which were easily transportable. Coins and medals were eminently collectible and portable, as were copies of ancient jewellery, cameos and impressed seals.

Coins were widely collected: here, a gold aureus of Hadrian, AD 134.

Decorated glass from Murano in Venice was popular, along with furniture, brooches and pictures made up of *pietra dura* or micro-mosaics. Tourists collected easy-to-carry items such as ornate *nécessaires* and richly decorated snuff boxes.

For other tourists, acquiring art was what mattered. Take the 2nd Earl of Egremont, who toured between 1727 and 1730. He developed a real collecting mania and appointed two agents in Rome with the specific task of purchasing works on his behalf. Between 1750 and 1760 he acquired some 70 statues and busts, many of them copies of

Greco-Roman originals. He also purchased over 200 paintings, displaying them at his magnificent home at Petworth in Sussex. His collection was further developed by his son who went on two Grand Tours in the 1770s, visiting Dresden, Paris, Berlin, Prague and Vienna, as well as Venice. He brought more than 250 paintings back to Petworth, including many painted by Grand Masters.

The tourists came from all over Britain, meaning that their influence when they returned was felt nationwide. Sir Watkin Williams-Wynn, 4th Baronet, had inherited a vast estate while still in his infancy. It was known as Wynnstay and was the largest country seat in North Wales. He conducted his Grand Tour in 1768, and was sculpted in Rome by Christopher Hewetson, a leading neoclassical sculptor of portrait busts. He returned to become a patron of art in Wales, commissioning artists such as Paul Sandby and Richard Wilson and inviting

George III penwork treasure chest containing intaglio seals, fossils, shells and geological specimens.

Double snuff box made of gold and brown agate, of French origin, c.1738.

A *nécessaire*, French-made, containing useful items such as tweezers, mirror, file and scent bottles, dating from the 1760s.

them to stay with him at Wynnstay. They helped develop the tradition of Welsh landscape painting. Sir Watkin also commissioned Robert Adam to design his London house at 20/21 St James's Square London, as well as employing Sir Joshua Reynolds to paint family portraits.

Other Grand Tourists simply returned with their own ideas about what constituted good taste. These ideas, about architectural styles and garden design, were then put into practice when they remodelled their country estates. For many tourists, what really mattered was not the physical mementoes they brought back, but the friendships, networking contacts and, indeed, ideas with which they returned. Soane has already been mentioned, and patrons such as Thomas Pitt (a politician who was a leading art collector and who later became Baron Camelford), the politician John Patteson, and Philip Yorke, 3rd Earl of Hardwicke, all befriended Soane while on their respective tours, and later employed him as their architect to design their dream homes and extensions.

Dublin-born James Caulfeild, later to become the 1st Earl of Charlemont, embarked on a Grand Tour which was to last nine years and which took in Italy, Greece, Turkey and Egypt. When he returned, he commissioned William Chambers, another Grand Tourist, to act as architect on the design of Charlemont House and also the chapel and public theatre in Trinity College, Dublin. Chambers went on to become a founder member of the Royal Academy and nowadays he is best remembered for the pagoda in Kew Gardens and for the design of Somerset House.

The royal family were not excluded from the Tour. Prince William Henry, who was the Duke of Gloucester and a younger brother of George III, made several trips to the Continent in the 1770s and returned with artworks which he had either bought or commissioned. As for the King, he had neither the time nor inclination to travel. He was, however, instructed fully in Italian art and culture by his mentor John Stuart, 3rd Earl of Bute, and possibly it was on his advice that he purchased a considerable number of Italian prints from agents acting for Cardinal Albani and from Joseph Smith, the British consul in Venice. Smith played a large part in popularising *vedute*, or views, of Venice especially by artists such as Canaletto. He facilitated the sale of dozens of paintings by Canaletto to wealthy travellers as well as persuading the artist to visit London in 1746. He also arranged for prints of the artist's works to be published and amassed a huge collection of art, sold to King George for the not-insignificant sum of £10,000.

It heralded a tradition of royal collecting, given a further boost by the Prince Regent, who was an often-overlooked patron of the arts and a great art collector, despite never having set foot on the Continent.

Some were inspired by what they learnt on their Tour to develop ideas which altered their entire career. The Scottish baronet Sir John Hall of Dunglass left Edinburgh University for his Grand Tour, travelled to Italy and observed lava flows on Mount Etna and saw the effects of erosion. This enabled him to develop his ideas about the formation of the Earth. He went on to become one of Scotland's most important geologists and was made President of the Royal Society of Edinburgh. His son John made his Grand Tour almost forty years after his father, visiting

Cameos made popular souvenirs, combining wearable jewellery with classical images. Here, the head of a satyr, made in Italy in the eighteenth century.

Case for a
travelling service,
made in France
in 1788.

James Caulfeild,
later to become
the 1st Earl of
Charlemont, in
a painting by
Pompeo Batoni
dating from
around 1753.

many of the same places; the journals of both father and son are held by the National Library of Scotland.

Another Tourist, but one in the very early years before the Grand Tour itinerary became formalised, was the Anglo-Irishman Robert Boyle. Back in 1641 he had left Eton and spent time in Florence. He returned imbued with a desire to carry out scientific research and went on to become one of the founders of modern chemistry.

A similar inspiration was felt by Edmund Gibbon, who departed on his Grand Tour in 1763, reached Rome the following year and realised that his destiny was to write *The History of the Decline and Fall of the Roman Empire*. The first of its six volumes came out in 1776. For men like this, the Grand Tour was an absolute life-changer.

ARTISTS AND PATRONAGE

WEALTHY YOUNG NOBLES travelling through Europe enjoyed a symbiotic relationship with the often-impoverished young artists of the day. The travellers wanted mementos of their journey and were keen to enhance their reputation as patrons, and to appear to be cultured cognoscenti who knew about art. For the young painter, the opportunity to study drawing and painting back in Britain was limited – the Royal Academy did not open its doors until 1768 and although people like Kneller and Hogarth ran private art schools in London, the numbers were small.

The young artist willing to travel could learn the *chiaroscuro* techniques mastered by Caravaggio, and be inspired by working alongside the leading Italian artists living in Rome, of whom Pompeo Batoni was perhaps the best known. The 1750s saw the development of neoclassicism, where Rome was the cradle of the new fashion for simplicity and symmetry. No wonder artists poured into the city, and during their stay fostered friendships with the style-setters who would become their employers when they returned to Britain.

For anyone living north of the border there were no adequate teaching facilities available in Scotland, and Italy was the obvious choice for aspiring artists. Here they could enrol in the *Academie de France* in Rome, or indeed in the *Accademia di San Luca* in the same city, and spend time drawing church interiors, sketching ruins from antiquity, and copying the styles of great artists such as Raphael and Michelangelo. There was a tight-knit Scottish community in the Strada Felice area of Rome, boosted after 1719 when the exiled Scottish Court moved to the city.

It was to Rome that the Scottish artist Allan Ramsay travelled in 1736. He chose the route by sea, and endured being robbed in Genoa as well as nearly drowning when his boat overturned. Ramsay returned to Rome in 1754, spending three years in Italy with his new wife, studying classical art, visiting archaeological sites, and earning a precarious living painting tourists. He made further visits to Italy and prospered as a portrait artist back in Britain, working both in Edinburgh and in London. He was a favourite of the King and as a result was appointed Principal Painter in Ordinary to George III. This entailed painting His Majesty on literally dozens of occasions and these portraits would then be presented to ambassadors and colonial governors. Although started by Ramsay, these royal portraits were often finished by members of his staff.

The Royal Scottish Academy holds a large collection of Ramsay's sketches.

The taste in landscapes changed in the second part of the eighteenth century, influenced in part by William Gilpin's book *Essay on Prints*; this was published in 1768 and introduced the idea of the picturesque – a set of rules for depicting nature and concentrating on composition. Artists were encouraged to 'improve' on nature by creating the sublime picture, by introducing features such as distant ruins, or overhanging trees to frame the view, or by omitting things to improve balance. The book coincided with a rapid increase in Grand Tour visitor numbers, especially to Rome.

Allan Ramsay's pastel sketch entitled *A Country Girl at Surrentum*.

The Artist and his Family, painted by Benjamin West.

A succession of artists went to Italy, with two notable exceptions being Thomas Gainsborough and John Constable, both of whom were resolutely home-grown. The American artist Benjamin West came to Britain before setting off on his Grand Tour in 1760. He made numerous copies of the original paintings he saw, particularly by Titian and Raphael. When he returned, he settled in Britain and ended up as the second President of the Royal Academy in 1792, following the death of Sir Joshua Reynolds.

The artist George Romney toured between 1772 and 1775. He is best remembered today for being the man who became obsessed with Emma Hart (later, the wife of Sir William Hamilton and the mistress of Horatio Nelson), painting her on over 60 occasions.

Scottish painters of note who visited Italy included the pastelist Archibald Skirving and also Katherine Read, who stayed in Venice between 1750 and 1753.

Richard Wilson was a Welsh artist who went to Italy in 1750 and stayed for seven years, specialising in painting idealised

OVERLEAF
British Gentlemen in Rome, c.1750 by Katherine Read, showing tourists against a background of Roman ruins.

A Cavern near Naples, painted by Joseph Wright.

Italianate scenes and landscapes based upon classical literature. He returned to become one of the first great landscape artists, and was credited by Constable as being a major influence. He took on Thomas Jones as a pupil, teaching him to paint landscapes in what was termed 'the grand manner' before Jones went to Italy and lived in Rome and Naples for several years.

The 40-year-old artist Joseph Wright set off for Italy in 1773, with his new (and pregnant) wife in tow. On his return to Britain he settled in Derby, his home town, and some of his finest paintings featured scientific experiments. Many of his paintings are on display at the Derby City Art Gallery.

Joseph Mallord William Turner travelled widely in Europe after visiting France and Switzerland in 1802. He visited Venice on numerous occasions, as well as travelling to Naples to see Vesuvius. Fascinated by the power of nature both on land and at sea, he has long been known as 'the painter of light'.

Others travelled further afield, such as the artist David Roberts, who had started off as a scene painter in Edinburgh.

Persuaded by Turner to concentrate on landscapes, he travelled extensively in Spain before heading for Egypt and the Holy Land, where he spent two years before returning in 1840. He brought back a huge collection of sketches and paintings of the monuments and views he encountered. He was then able to raise advance subscriptions to pay for a series of lithographs to be prepared, publishing them as *Sketches* throughout the 1840s. He also travelled twice to Italy and in 1841 was elected as a member of the Royal Academy.

Joshua Reynolds toured Italy between 1750 and 1752, and it was Reynolds, more than anyone else, who emerged as the champion of classical Italian art, with an insistence that his pupils should study his heroes Caravaggio and Raphael. Reynolds had been one of the earliest members of the Royal Society of Arts and assisted in the formation of the Society of

Venice from the Porch of Madonna della Salute by J.M.W. Turner.

Lithograph by David Roberts: *The Temple at Dendur, Nubia.*

Artists of Great Britain, but really sealed his prominence when he became the first president of the Royal Academy of Arts in 1768. He emphasised the importance of the 'grand style' and believed that the only pictures with any value were those that adhered to strict rules laid down by him in a series of *Discourses*, which he delivered to students at the Royal Academy.

Reynolds became the most famous portrait painter of the second half of the eighteenth century, raising portraiture to the level of importance previously enjoyed by historical and religious works. He particularly favoured showing his sitters in poses painted by earlier classical and Renaissance artists.

RIGHT
Detail from portrait of the sculptress Anne Seymour Damer, painted in 1773 by Sir Joshua Reynolds.

FAR RIGHT
Detail from portrait of Mrs Abington as Miss Prue in *Love for Love* by William Congreve, painted by Reynolds in 1771.

It wasn't just painters who fancied a Roman holiday – sculptors found the experience invaluable. Joseph Wilton stayed in Rome for seven years, learning to master marble sculpting techniques in the 1750s. Joseph Nollekens had studied and worked as an antiques dealer, restorer and copier in Rome before returning to London in 1770. He became famous and was one of the most fashionable portrait sculptors in Britain. Anne Seymour Damer travelled extensively throughout Europe before being described as a 'female genius' by Horace Walpole, and he left her a life interest in Strawberry Hill House after his death in 1797. Thomas Banks was a sculptor who spent much of the 1770s in Rome, having obtained a travel scholarship from the Royal Academy.

Detail from Thomas Rowlandson's *The Sculptor*, showing Joseph Nollekens sculpting Venus, 1800.

Nollekens' bust of William Pitt the Younger, based on his death mask.

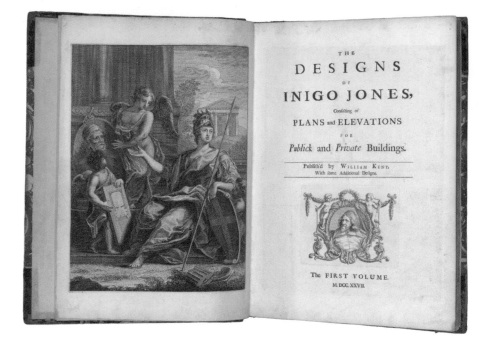

THE
DESIGNS
OF
INIGO JONES,
Consisting of
PLANS and ELEVATIONS
FOR
Publick and *Private* Buildings.

Publish'd by WILLIAM KENT,
With some Additional Designs.

The FIRST VOLUME.
M. DCC. XXVII.

William Kent's book on Inigo Jones, published in 1727.

In 1610, way before the Grand Tour had become standard, the young Earl of Arundel set off for Rome and Naples in the company of a 40-year-old architect called Inigo Jones. Their tour was profoundly important. For the Earl it launched a passion for collecting, and for Inigo Jones it led to a detailed study of the works of Andrea Palladio, who had published a treatise entitled *The Four Books of Architecture* in 1570. Influenced by this, Jones went on to produce radical new ideas which transformed British architecture, starting with his designs for the Queen's House at Greenwich and the Banqueting Hall, Whitehall. In 1714 William Kent travelled to Italy and it was in Vicenza that he studied the works of Andrea Palladio and through this began to appreciate the significance of Inigo Jones. In 1727 he published a highly influential book entitled *The Designs of Inigo Jones* and its success led to what was known as the Palladian style being reflected in designs for country houses and villas across Britain.

Kent's influence can best be seen at Houghton Hall and Holkham Hall, both in Norfolk. He also remodelled many existing buildings, including those at Rousham House in Oxford, Badminton House in Gloucestershire and the interiors of Burlington House and Chiswick House in London.

Another of the leading neoclassical architects was Robert Adam, who had spent five years on the Continent studying architecture after first visiting Rome in 1752. Robert Adam and his brother James combined to define the 'Adam style' which dominated tastes between 1760 and 1795, before giving way to Regency and then French Empire style. The style of the Adam brothers involved integrating all aspects of the design of the house, from the actual building to all the interiors. Walls, ceilings, fireplaces, furniture, fixtures, fittings and carpets were all designed as part of a single uniform scheme.

His great rival within the neoclassical movement was James Wyatt, who studied for six years in Italy. He was elected to the Royal Academy in 1785 and was its president from 1805 to 1806.

The point to make is that all of these artistic visitors were not wealthy enough to be part of the actual Grand Tour: they were hangers on, either fighting for scraps doled out by the wealthier visitors, making contacts which would be invaluable back home, or simply mastering the style which their clients would regard as 'cutting edge' when it came to building and kitting out their new country houses.

Robert Adam's design for one end of the parlour at Headfort House, Ireland, 1771.

THE ENGLISH COUNTRY HOUSE

While the Palladian movement had developed in the late Stuart and early Georgian period, it had done so alongside a taste for baroque architecture, with its ornate swirls, curves and ornamentation which copied the ornate palaces visited on European tours. Blenheim Palace and Castle Howard, both built to the designs of Sir John Vanbrugh, are fine examples of the baroque style, alongside Chatsworth and the Old Royal Naval College, which was built at Greenwich between 1696 and 1712.

However, after 1730 a return to the strict interpretation of the ancient buildings of Greece and Rome led to the neoclassical movement – more austere than Palladian, less influenced by Renaissance ideals.

Perhaps the first neoclassical building in England was started in 1709 by the amateur architect William Benson, a landowner in Wiltshire. He did his Grand Tour, liked what he saw in Germany and Italy, and decided to try his hand at designing Wilbury House, with its arrangement of columns that adhere to classical architectural orders and its triangular, temple-like pediment. From then on, as each young blade returned from his own Continental tour having seen 'the real thing', he resolved to change his ancestral home to follow neoclassical lines.

In the case of Chatsworth it was the 1st Duke of Devonshire who went on a Grand Tour, returning in 1661 with the ambition to remodel the Elizabethan mansion. He rebuilt the

OPPOSITE
Castle Howard,
Yorkshire,
designed by Sir
John Vanbrugh in
dramatic baroque
style.

Sir John Vanbrugh's design for the front elevation of Kings Weston House at Bristol, 1710.

William Hogarth's portrait of William Cavendish, Marquess of Hartington, later 4th Duke of Devonshire, painted in 1741.

East Front, which includes the Painted Hall and Long Gallery. Between 1699 and 1702 he added the West Front and managed to complete the North Front just before he died in 1707.

The next two dukes built up the magnificent collection of paintings and sculptures, and when the title passed to the 4th Duke, he visited Italy between 1739 and 1740, accompanied by his tutor, the Reverend Arthur Smyth. A generation later the man destined to become the 5th Duke repeated the Italian Tour, this time with William Fitzherbert. He married Lady Georgiana Spencer and their son, who was to become 6th Duke, continued the family tradition and became a regular visitor to Italy. He built a new wing, which included a dining room, orangery, private theatre and sculpture gallery. He used this to house his magnificent collection of sculptures, widely accepted as being the most impressive in the country in private hands.

In 1729 at the age of 19, Lord John Russell travelled through Europe accompanied by his tutor. In 1744, as 4th Duke of Bedford, he started rebuilding the old Cistercian abbey in Bedfordshire which his family had owned for many years, replacing it with the present structure known as Woburn Abbey. With its magnificent art collection, it is still in private ownership.

Other architects who never got as far as going on their own Grand Tour quickly learned that the way to get commissions was to follow the direction taken by the likes of William Kent. In the case of Roger Morris, he designed a Palladian villa for the Countess of Suffolk, mistress to King George II, in 1729. Known as Marble Hill House, Twickenham, it now belongs to English Heritage and is open to the public. The design became so popular

John Buckler's view of the South-west elevation of Chatsworth House in 1812.

because of its symmetry and simple lines that it was quickly adopted as a template for other English villas. Although he produced plans for many Palladian houses, including one for Whitton House, shown here, Morris also experimented with what was to become the Gothic Revival style, designing Clearwell Castle in Gloucestershire as early as 1727.

It was only after he had achieved success that Morris got to travel to Italy, in 1731/2, accompanied by his patron George Bubb Dodington. Morris went on to design several houses for Dodington before his death in 1749.

In the case of Nathaniel Curzon his Grand Tour only took him to France and the Low Countries, but when he returned, he vowed to produce a home to rival his near neighbours in

A design by Roger Morris showing an elevation of Whitton House, Middlesex, c.1732.

Sir James Dashwood, painted when he was 23 by Enoch Seeman.

Derbyshire, the Cavendishes of Chatsworth. Curzon commissioned Robert Adam to design Kedleston Hall with its magnificent hall lined with Corinthian columns, and the saloon with a dome imitating the Pantheon in Rome. Here he housed his sculpture collection. The house now belongs to the National Trust.

At the age of 19, James Dashwood was enjoying himself on his Grand Tour when he inherited a baronetcy along with thousands of acres of prime Oxford countryside. He returned and commissioned the building of Kirtlington Park. The result was a stunning Palladian mansion, set in grounds laid out by Capability Brown. Nowadays it is an exclusive wedding venue, the rococo dining room having been dismantled and moved to the Metropolitan Museum in New York in 1931. The house was built between 1742 and 1746, largely to the design of John Sanderson, a London-based architect who specialised in giving the returning tourists what they were looking for at this point in time – Palladian with a touch of rococo flair.

Sometimes a landowner 'bought in' ideas without actually going on the Tour. An example of this was at Stourhead, where the banker Henry Hoare used his huge wealth to build the obligatory Palladian house and then set it off with a magnificent garden complete with a man-made lake, temples, grottoes and an Arcadian cottage. His grandson was the one to get to go on the Tour, twice, returning with a fine art collection which he housed in two new wings to the house. Ironically, those two wings were the only parts not damaged by the fire which ripped through Stourhead House in 1902. Since rebuilt, the house and gardens are now maintained by the National Trust.

Another building commissioned without involving a Tour was at Croome Court in Worcestershire. The Earl of Coventry

The Dining
Room at
Kirtlington.

inherited the land and commissioned Capability Brown to
design the garden. Brown may never have gone on the Tour
himself, but his landscape design reflected many features
borrowed from Italian villas. He moved an entire village and
built a church just so that the view from the house would be

The Tapestry
Room from
Croome Court,
now to be seen
in New York's
Metropolitan
Museum.

A View of the Grotto & Two Shell Temples, the gardens at Stowe.

enhanced. He even designed the house itself, in Palladian style, and most of the property is now owned by the National Trust. The original Tapestry Room is missing, because it was dismantled and moved to New York, including the plasterwork ceilings designed by a young Robert Adam at the start of his career, together with the tapestries which had been commissioned direct from the factory in Gobelins, France.

Brown transformed hundreds of English gardens. His work is evident at Stowe House, now a public school but with the grounds belonging to the National Trust. It exemplifies the idea of a 'natural' garden, albeit littered with Doric temples, classical sculptures, lakes, Palladian bridges and follies. With its house designed by a succession of architects, including John Vanbrugh, William Kent and Robert Adam, Stowe became the centre of a sort of 'reverse Grand Tour', with Continental visitors coming to Buckinghamshire to visit what was seen as the quintessential English country estate, built to the orders of Lord Cobham.

Other gardens owed more to the particular person who went on the tour, a case in point being George, 1st Baron Lyttleton. As a politician he was to become Chancellor of the Exchequer, but as a landscape gardener he spent years developing the parkland at Hagley Hall, which he built near Kidderminster to the designs of Sanderson Miller, the pioneer of Gothic Revival architecture. The grounds reflected Lyttleton's love of literature, with its numerous statues erected to honour literary figures, as well as an obelisk, temple and a folly built to look like a ruined medieval castle.

Overall, the eighteenth century was the Golden Age of the country house. With their roots firmly in Ancient Greece and Rome, and with their inspiration in the Grand Tour, buildings such as the ones featured here have never lost their appeal.

WOMEN ON TOUR

IT WOULD BE a mistake to believe that the Grand Tour was limited to young men. Women also completed Grand Tours, though in far smaller numbers and often for very different reasons. There is a distinction between female tourists and female Grand Tourists. In the former category might be women who travelled to Paris in order to acquire the latest fashions, an example being the courtesan Mary Robinson, who fled to the French capital in October 1781 to lick her wounds after being dumped by the Prince of Wales. She went back regularly, each time returning to London sporting the very latest in French *haute couture*. Another tourist was a different courtesan, Elizabeth Armistead, who toured Europe for nearly a year, returning to England in 1782. She was accompanied by a string of titled patrons. Her former lover, Lord Derby, took her to Paris and then to Spa in Belgium to take the waters. Later she was accompanied by the Earl of Cholmondeley to Italy, then by Lord Coleraine back to Paris. Twenty years later she accompanied her husband, the politician Charles James Fox, when he went to Paris to be presented to the Emperor Napoleon in 1802.

Then there were the women who fled to France to escape their creditors – such

Italian-made fan from 1786 showing scenes of antiquity and, in the centre, Mount Vesuvius erupting.

A caricature by James Gillray dated 1801, entitled *A Cognocenti contemplating ye Beauties of ye Antique*. It shows the connoisseur Sir William Hamilton in old age, inspecting his collection of sculptures including those of his wife Emma Hamilton.

as Dorothea Jordan, an actress who had been the mistress of the Duke of Clarence for 21 years, bearing at least ten children by him, before being unceremoniously dropped by her royal lover. She moved to Boulogne, where she died in abject poverty in 1816. Another exile was Seymour Fleming, who fled abroad to avoid the scandal of her numerous affairs, while married to Sir Richard Worsley, 7th Baronet. Other women travelled with their husbands – Emma Hamilton moving to Naples in 1786 to be with Sir William Hamilton, whom she married five years later. Another woman living in exile was Nancy Parsons. She was the one-time mistress of the Duke of Grafton, and went on to marry the 2nd Viscount Maynard, some ten years her junior. They lived in Naples, where she then embarked on a *ménage à trois* with the teenage 5th Duke of Bedford, in a very public display which would never have been accepted had she stayed in Britain.

All these women were tainted by scandal, to one degree or another. But the female Grand Tourists were cut from a very different cloth. Theirs were no debauched travels. Unlike many of their male counterparts they did not spend vast fortunes on acquiring souvenirs or stripping archaeological sites. They toured for a far more exalted purpose – to broaden their minds. Constrained by Society's ingrained misogyny, prevented from obtaining a decent education and barred from most professional jobs, these determined ladies must have been astonished to find countries where women were free to express opinions. In Italy they could hear about the physicist Laura Bassi who, in 1732, became the world's first female professor. In France they could be inspired by Emilie du Châtelet, a brilliant mathematician who translated Newton's *Principia* from Latin into French in 1749. Grand Tourists could attend *salons* in Paris and hear other women debate issues of the day. When those intrepid travellers returned to Britain, they were able to become *salonnières* themselves, arranging meetings for anyone interested in stimulating conversation. Some became known as blue-stockings, a name which included men and women alike, and they provided an antidote to the male-only societies and clubs which dominated the era. Women started to question the strait-jackets imposed on them and to demand greater rights and freedoms – the right to vote, freedom to think and to express opinions, freedom to travel. The logical conclusion of this was the decision by Mary Wollstonecraft to move to Paris to experience the excitement of the period of change associated with the French Revolution. She ended up writing *A Vindication of the Rights of Woman* in 1790, one of the most important books of the early feminist movement.

Other women looked to inspire stay-at-home followers by writing about their experiences, with the first significant travel writer being Lady Mary Wortley Montagu. She had travelled to the Ottoman Empire in 1717 as the wife of the British ambassador and she subsequently wrote of her experiences in her *Turkish Embassy Letters*. She visited Italy on three occasions, but her letters describing her Italian experiences were published without her authority. In 1776 Lady Anna Miller published *Letters from Italy*, describing a visit which she made with her husband and detailing Italian art and culture for the benefit of armchair travellers. Then, in 1800 Mariana Starke wrote her *Letters from Italy*. It acted as a guide for others, especially after the letters were re-issued as part of a general European travel guide, complete with recommended packing lists and handy tips for travellers.

DRAWBACKS AND DOWNSIDES

THE PUBLIC BACK in Britain would no doubt argue that the worst thing that came out of the Grand Tour was the fashion for wearing ludicrous clothes and the affected mannerisms displayed by the oh-so-dedicated followers of fashion. No matter that the wearer may never have been on the Tour himself, he wanted everyone to believe that he was a well-travelled, cultured, gentleman – and that meant adopting macaroni fashions.

A more serious downside of the Grand Tour was the cost: the outflow of possibly millions of pounds annually from Britain to Europe was regarded as harmful to the national economy. Economists raged at the extravagance.

On a personal scale, the cost to individual families could be enormous. Living abroad for, say, four years, staying in rented apartments and hotels, was extremely expensive. Of course, the traveller could economise by eating simple fare in coffee houses, or have food prepared by his own servants, but if he aspired to mix freely with his wealthier companions, he would have to face exorbitant charges for fine banquets in grand houses.

It was a tradition that on arrival in Paris a complete wardrobe in clothes would be bought, since French fashion was considered far in advance of anything available in London. The cost of buying a carriage was prohibitive to all but the very rich, but the alternative meant constantly paying for stage coaches and privately hired vehicles. Advance

OPPOSITE
The macaroni painter, or, Billy Dimple sitting for his picture shows the artist Richard Cosway having his portrait painted in 1772. Both sitter and artist are shown wearing flamboyant and dandified dress.

Journey by Sedan Chair, 1828, by an unknown artist.

booking for rooms, whether for weeks or maybe months, could result in a substantial discount, but travellers arriving on spec would find the accommodation cost greatly inflated. And all payments involved money changing, where typically one per cent was creamed off by the correspondent bank or money changer. Then there were the avoidable expenses, starting with the cost of acquiring and crating home huge quantities of souvenirs, whether in the form of statuary, ancient artefacts, paintings or furniture.

Detail from *Portrait of a Young Man*, painted by Pompeo Batoni.

Much as distant parents and travelling tutors might protest, some of the tourists were content to finance entire excavations by purchasing the necessary licences. Bribes paid to officials to turn a blind eye to the unauthorised removal of artefacts from countries such as Italy were commonplace.

The volume of goods sent back to Britain was staggering: all those newly built country homes needed filling. Here on the Grand Tour the homeowner could buy his paintings by the yard, his sculptures by the crate, and know that by the time he headed for home he would have a mansion filled with items which would demonstrate his connoisseurship. In an era before selfies, the traveller would have his portrait painted with recognisable ruins in the background – for instance the Colosseum. It was a sort of 'I was there – and I have the picture to prove it.' Italian portrait painters did not come cheap…

But these excesses were nothing compared to the pleasures of the flesh enjoyed by many of the participants on the Grand Tour. Just out of their teens, away from parental control, the tourists really hit their stride by the time they reached Venice. Having endured the punishing regime of polishing up social skills in Paris, here was a chance for the Grand Tourist to let rip – and he did so with a vengeance. Venetian courtesans were renowned for being both brazen and beautiful. For some, Florence was a particular eye-opener with its catamites – rent boys – touting for business. Back in 1641 the English chemist Robert Boyle had commented how even the monks were sexually avaricious, calling them 'gowned sodomites … with goatish heats' when he encountered them in a local brothel.

An English-made travelling medicine cabinet, dating from 1830.

Whether it was Lord Byron with his affair with a married Venetian lady, or James Boswell moving from one libidinous encounter to the next, Italy was the place to over-indulge. The result of all this promiscuity was that there was an epidemic of sexually transmitted diseases. These would be brought back to Britain, where effective treatments did not exist. As a result, syphilis and gonorrhoea were rampant throughout the Georgian period.

For some of their Lordships, the sexual side of the Tour was what it was all about: why bother with all those old ruins when there was fun to be had? Take Sir Henry Fetherstonhaugh, 2nd Baronet, who embarked on his Grand Tour at the age of 21. He spent most of his Tour bed-hopping his way through Europe.

The Tour over, he returned to his estate at Uppark in West Sussex where, as a party animal, he quickly earned the reputation of being a 'witless playboy'. He installed the teenager Emma Hart as his mistress and Emma threw herself into her role as party hostess with energy and enthusiasm. Hooray Henry then got Emma pregnant and he chucked her out. Emma later went on to be the mistress of Lord Nelson while also being the wife of Sir William Hamilton in Naples.

Meanwhile, Sir Henry waited until he was 71 before he finally settled down. He married his chief dairy maid, 50 years his junior. The couple lived in apparent harmony for 21 years, and when Sir Henry died, he left his widow the house at Uppark. With an adult life like that, you could say that the Grand Tour was a marvellous training ground …

For others, the Tour gave a different opportunity to explore sexuality and to take part in homosexual activities which were still capital offences back in Britain. As a young man, William Beckford was described as being the richest person in the country. In 1777 at the age of 17 he left on his version of the Grand Tour, making a second one, to Venice, in 1780. In both cases he returned after embarking on well-publicised homosexual affairs. Beckford then started on a tour of Britain, got as far as Powderham Castle near Exeter, and started an affair with William 'Kitty' Courtenay, then a boy barely into his teens.

When the couple were caught *in flagrante*, Beckford fled the country and settled in Switzerland, not returning to Britain until 1795. He remained a social outcast for the rest of his life. The unfortunate Kitty Courtenay was forced into exile and never returned to Britain.

This is not of course to say that homosexuality was a 'downside' of the Tour – but the Tour gave young men the opportunity to dream and hope for a more tolerant society, and ultimately that led to a great deal of disappointment when they came home to reality.

Gambling and excessive drinking were other common features of the Tour, and for many, if their health and wealth were not ruined during the Tour, it was to be their downfall once they returned to Britain, where gambling and alcoholism were endemic.

Classical Landscape with Ruins, in the style of Robert Adam.

One other concern about the Tour for families was that their sons would be trapped into 'unfortunate' marriages. 'Unfortunate' would include unions with gold-digging females, but also girls from Roman Catholic families. To the average Englishman, Catholic-controlled France and Italy represented something dangerous and abhorrent, not least because Catholics were associated with the Jacobites, who were intent on overthrowing the House of Hanover. And of course, such unions may indeed have taken place, as with the Duke of Sussex, ninth child of George III, who went to Rome in 1793 and fell for the charms of Lady Augusta Murray. She was the daughter of the 4th Earl of Dunmore, a Catholic who was an avowed supporter of 'Bonnie Prince Charlie'. They went through a form of marriage ceremony – invalid under the terms of the Royal Marriages Act – and the King had to send a minister to Italy to haul them back to face the music. And if that could happen to royalty, it could happen to anyone.

Some were left with a dim view of what they saw on Tour, with Horace Walpole describing Paris with the words: 'It is the

ugliest, beastliest town in the universe.' To Benjamin Robert Haydon it was a 'filthy hole' and to the travel writer Philip Thicknesse it was 'a melancholy residence for a stranger who neither plays at cards, dice, or deals in the principal manufacture of the city: ready-made love.'

The poet Percy Bysshe Shelley didn't think much of the people he met in Italy either, writing: 'The people here, though inoffensive enough, seem both in body and soul a miserable race. The men are hardly men; they look like a tribe of stupid and shrivelled slaves, and I do not think that I have seen a gleam of intelligence in the countenance of man since I passed the Alps.' Meanwhile an early seventeenth-century traveller to Venice by the name of Thomas Coryat spoke of '2,000 courtesans in the city, whereof many are esteemed so loose that they are said to open their quiver to every arrow.' Edward Gibbon was unimpressed with the architecture in Venice, writing to a friend, 'Of all the towns in Italy, I am the least satisfied with Venice … Old and in general ill-built houses, ruined pictures, and stinking ditches dignified with the pompous denomination of Canals; a fine bridge, spoilt by two rows of houses upon it, and a large square decorated with the worst architecture I ever yet saw.'

It is a reminder that on the Grand Tour, one man's meat was another man's poison.

FURTHER READING

BOOKS

Black, Jeremy. *The British Abroad: The Grand Tour in the Eighteenth Century.* Sutton Publishing Ltd, 1992.

Dolan, Brian. *Ladies of the Grand Tour.* Flamingo, 2002.

Hibbert, Christopher. *The Grand Tour.* Thames Methuen, 1987.

O'Loughlin Katrina. *Women, Writing, and Travel in the Eighteenth Century.* Cambridge University Press, 2018.

Sweet, Rosemary. *Cities and the Grand Tour: The British in Italy c.1690–1820.* Cambridge University Press, 2012.

ONLINE RESOURCES

Amblard, Marion. The Scottish painters' exile in Italy in the eighteenth century. https://journals.openedition.org/etudesecossaises/219

Brown, Iain (National Library of Scotland). The Grand Tour. https://www.youtube.com/watch?v=Pv9al35xtsA

Burk, Kathleen. The Grand Tour of Europe (Gresham College lecture). https://www.gresham.ac.uk/lectures-and-events/the-grand-tour-of-europe

Chaliakopoulos, Antonis. 12 famous art collectors of Britain in the 16th–19th centuries. https://www.thecollector.com/12-famous-art-collectors-of-britain-in-the-16-19th-centuries/

Figes, Lydia. Decoding the Grand Tour portraits of Pompeo Batoni. https://artuk.org/discover/stories/decoding-the-grand-tour-portraits-of-pompeo-batoni

Knowles, Rachel. Regency History – The Grand Tour. https://www.regencyhistory.net/2013/04/the-grand-tour.html

National Trust. What was the Grand Tour? https://www.nationaltrust.org.uk/petworth-house-and-park/features/what-was-the-grand-tour

Sorabella, Jean. Essay on the Grand Tour, for the
    Metropolitan Museum of Art. https://www.metmuseum.
    org/toah/hd/grtr/hd_grtr.htm

PLACES TO VISIT

ENGLAND

Bowood House, Old Road, Derry Hill, Calne SN11 0LZ.
    Telephone: 01249 812102. Website: www.bowood.org

Castle Howard, York YO60 7DA. Telephone: 01653
    648621. Website: www.castlehoward.co.uk

Kedleston Hall, near Quarndon, Derby, Derbyshire
    DE22 5JH. Telephone: 01332 842191.
    Website: www.nationaltrust.org.uk/kedleston-hall

Knole House, Sevenoaks, Kent TN15 0RP. Telephone: 0344
    249 1895. Website: www.nationaltrust.org.uk/knole

Powderham Castle, Kenton, Exeter EX6 8JQ.
    Telephone: 01626 890243. Website:
    www.powderham.co.uk

Stourhead, Stourton, Warminster, Wiltshire BA12 6QF.
    Telephone: 01747 841152. Website: www.nationaltrust.
    org.uk/stourhead

Stowe, New Inn Farm, Buckingham MK18 5EQ.
    Telephone: 01280 817156. Website:
    www.nationaltrust/org.uk/stowe

Strawberry Hill House, 268 Waldegrave Road, Twickenham
    TW1 4ST. Telephone: 020 8744 1241. Website:
    www.strawberryhillhouse.org.uk

Tatton Hall, Mereheath Drive, Knutsford WA16 6SG.
    Telephone: 01625 374400. Website: www.tattonpark.org.uk

Towneley Hall, Towneley Park, Holmes Street, Burnley
    BB11 3RQ. Telephone: 01282 477130. Website:
    www.towneley.org.uk

Uppark, South Harting, Petersfield, West Sussex
GU31 5QR. Telephone: 01730 825415. Website:
www.nationaltrust.org.uk/uppark-house-and-garden
Wilton House, Wilton, Salisbury SP2 0BJ. Telephone: 01722
746714. Website: www.wiltonhouse.co.uk

WALES

Plas Newydd House, Llanfairpwll, Anglesey LL61 6DQ.
Telephone: 01248 714795. Website: www.nationaltrust.
org.uk/plas-newydd-house-and-garden
Tredegar House, Pencarn Way, Newport NP10 8YW.
Telephone: 0344 249 1895. Website: www.nationaltrust.
org.uk/tredegar-house

SCOTLAND

Hopetoun House, South Queensferry, Edinburgh
EH30 9RW. Telephone: 0131 331 2451.
Website: www.hopetoun.co.uk
Mellerstain House, Gordon, Scottish Borders TD3 6LG.
Telephone: 01573 410225. Website: www.
mellerstain.com
Newhailes House, Musselburgh, East Lothian EH21 6RY.
Telephone: 0131 653 5599. Website: www.nts.org.uk/
visit/places/newhailes

NORTHERN IRELAND

Hillsborough Castle, The Square, Hillsborough BT26 6AG.
Telephone: 0333 320 6000. Website: www.hrp.org.uk/
hillsborough-castle

INDEX